WHITE ALBUM

WHITE ALBUM

poems by Rishma Dunlop *& paintings by* Suzanne Northcott

inanna poetry & fiction series

INANNA Publications and Education Inc.
Toronto, Canada

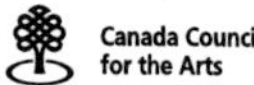 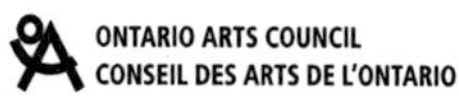

We gratefully acknowledge the support of the Canada Council
for the Arts and the Ontario Arts Council for our publishing program.

We are also grateful for the support received
from an Anonymous Fund at The Calgary Foundation. 

We acknowledge the support of LindaLando Fine Art towards
the colour reproductions in this volume.

Library and Archives Canada Cataloguing in Publication

Dunlop, Rishma, 1956-
     White album : poems / by Rishma Dunlop; paintings by
Suzanne Northcott.

(Inanna poetry & fiction series)
ISBN 978-0-9808822-3-0

     I. Title. II. Series: Inanna poetry and fiction series

PS8557.U53995W45 2008   C811'.6   C2008-906372-4

Cover design by Val Fullard
Interior design by Luciana Ricciutelli
Printed and bound in Canada

Inanna Publications and Education Inc.
210 Founders College, York University
4700 Keele Street, Toronto, Ontario M3J 1P3 Canada
Telephone: (416) 736-5356 Fax (416) 736-5765
Email: inanna@yorku.ca Website: www.yorku.ca/inanna

Suzanne Northcott and Rishma Dunlop have a long history of artistic collaborations including art installations at private and public galleries, invited lectures, performances, and publications. In 2002, Northcott and Dunlop collaborated on their first exhibition, "The Body of My Garden" at LindaLando Fine Art, coinciding with the launch of Dunlop's book of poems by the same title. They have published numerous collaborative articles in *Language and Literacy, Poeisis, International Artists' Magazine,* and a limited edition chapbook *The Blue Hour* in 2004. Exhibitions include "Crossing Boundary" at the Surrey Public Art Gallery in 2005, and "Esperanza" at Linda-Lando Fine Art in 2007. *White Album* was launched in 2008 as part of Suzanne Northcott's exhibition "Lucid Ground," at LindaLando Fine Art.

"Bracketed by the violence of the turbulent 1960s and our current violence of terrorism and the war in Iraq, this extraordinary collection of poetry draws us into the life of a Canadian woman of Indian descent as she grows up in a hybrid world where she helps her father wrap his turban each morning and yet sings along with him to "An English Country Garden"; where she marries in a sari, yet grooves to Motown and irons her hair to look like Ali McGraw in *Love Story*. The collection is also luminously inflected with loss the death of her father, the loss of her innocence, the loss of her daughters as they take up their own trajectories. Rishma Dunlop's work, in the vein of writers like Wayson Choy and Judy Fong Bates, documents the life of those who were multicultural when Canada was overwhelmingly white and Anglo-Saxon. *White Album* speaks for that silent generation. By using the medium of poetry, Dunlop brings such a knife-like precision of language, such a concentrated clarity of image, to the life documented that it remains seared indelibly into our minds."

—Shyam Selvadurai, author of *Funny Boy*

"Each lucid image shines in Rishma Dunlop's fourth book of poems, *White Album*. Sometimes mournful, sometimes full of sass, her poems come marbled with song lyrics, and blended both with memories of a suburban girl's coming of age and coming to grips with her heritage. Dunlop achieves her crystalline power by directing a bright white light on all her manifold subjects. Here is a poet who, with muscle, grace, and even a discography, fearlessly focuses on the contradictions of her time."

—Molly Peacock, author of *Second Blush*

"In *White Album*, the paintings of Suzanne Northcott provide a provocative counterpoint and dialogue with the poetic texts. Northcott's images are evidence of a unique way of seeing the human figure alongside abstract vistas of contemporary colour fields. Poignant and powerful, these paintings engage the viewer in visceral perceptions of spatial and temporal readings of selves and the world. A painter at the height of her talents, Northcott renders visible the tenuous, fragile nature of identities and the tentativeness of memory, all the while remaining connected to the joyousness of human existence."

—Linda Lando, LindaLando Fine Art

Contents

Driving Home With Chet

Chet Baker on the stereo –
I imagine his Caravaggio face, heroin-
ruined in the single spot, as the horn comes
into languor, slow notes suffusing the groin –

applause for the trumpet's blue arrangements,
eighth notes slurring past slate roofs,
scatter-shots of sounds, familiar and strange –
cry of sirens, construction cranes –

kids playing at dusk, falling into their
own shadows on lawns like scissors –
metronomed scales of piano practice,
staccato of footsteps, coming home –

above the trumpet's metal and spit,
refrigerator hum, the din of phones,
someone coughs, someone hisses a white rage
for the song gone out of their bones –

ignition keyed quiet, Chet's last notes –
long vibrato shaping pain into order,
in the last crease of light –
thin as a knife,
a wish.

Evening Fields VIII, 2002

1

Outside in the distance a wildcat did growl,
Two riders were approaching and the wind began to howl

—Bob Dylan, "All Along the Watchtower"

Vigil for Resident Aliens

Thousands cross borders—
each late arrival a ceremony

to announce how far they've travelled.
Language a bruise, roots in parcels,

the smell of miles on their clothes—
countless white nights of insomnia

that kept the roofs from falling.
Citizens become aliens

women's veils become partitions.
Turbaned men drive taxis,

English a raw tangle of verbs
in their thick accents—

not my parents' Queen's English.
Passports are fingered nervously

with every border-crossing,

every honour killing

of some disobedient bride.
Imagine then,

a descant.
A glass of cool water,

quiet.

Journey

In the aftermath of the empire's death —
trains cross the border between Pakistan and India,
spilling bodies and severed hands of Sikhs, Hindus, Muslims.
Mother escapes with what she could carry
across the split world from Lahore,
as Kashmir became Partition's open sore.

In the aftermath of my birth,
my first days lit by bulbs
of white jasmine,
the world spread wide before my parents.
They take what is at hand — father's scientific journals,
mother's rose-strewn Kashmiri shawls.

They pack their bags,
read the guidebooks,
and follow the lines that lead us
from the warm palm of empire
to its furthest frost-bitten fingertips.

Molting Rose, 2007

11

Molting Petals, 2007

The Colour of Home

Home is a white pocket of Englishness,
a neighbourhood named for a lord of Her Highness,

in Montréal where I chant skipping songs
about girls who resemble English roses,

where I double-dutch and hula-hoop on suburban lawns,
where I roller-skate down Avondale Road,

while mother hollers
and hollers me home.

At school I turn white when teacher asks me to write
on the blackboard and the sleeve of my white

blouse blurs another's answers.
Mother gets me excused from Bible study

but I still recite prayers
and sing to the painted face

of Her Majesty every day. The sentences I write –
about nation and God and country –

enter me.

Love Field, 1963

As usual, father woke me
for the daily ritual that required
each of us to grip one end
of starched burgundy muslin
and stretch until, satisfied,
he folded the lengths up and tied
the newly made (like magic) turban
round his long black hair,
then kissed me on the forehead, there,
then disappeared briefcase in hand
out the front door. On school holidays
I loved to visit him at work,
which was Ayerst Laboratories
with the beakers and all
the way downtown by train,
and how he would have me shrieking
when he flicked that gleaming
pink liquid at my blouse –
the stuff that vanished
like stains in Cheer commercials.
He always made sure to wear
while I was there

the white lab coat I loved.

That morning, though,
I dressed myself in white
blouse and knee-socks
packed my bookbag
and went sighing to school,
my nose in *Charlotte's Web.*
Mother planned dinner
by menus in *Good Housekeeping.*

When I came home, I found mother
in the family room ironing
and watching TV and ironing.
This soap was new, not *As the World
Turns,* but the woman beside herself
with a bouquet of roses, beside her
husband in the Lincoln
moving past the Texas Schoolbook
Depository to Dealey Plaza, Dallas,
the open motorcade,
the gunshots, and the scene replayed –

the woman in the proper pink suit
and pillbox hat waving a white gloved hand.

Suddenly I realized mother was crying
her whole chest heaving,
something I'd never seen before
and it scared me. I was seven years old
and wanted it to stop,
this weeping that was large and lungful.

That's how father found us in the family room,
amidst mother's ironing,
her pink slip and pedal pushers and pink sari,
her Maidenform girdles and bras,
the pink sleeveless dress and matching coat
she bought me
at Ogilvy's Department Store,
all that pink scattered on the floor
and spattered on the floor
of the Lincoln
and the TV still going.
He put his briefcase down

and she held him
or was held. Then, with me, he unwound
his turban, turned it back
to burgundy, to pure colour
that could be put away.
That night, in the suburbs of the West Island,
in Beaconsfield, Quebec,
while the white chalk of hopscotch
games ghosted the streets,
my parents watched the evening news before bed
as was their custom. And they are still there
in the hours before midnight –
the woman with her husband
in his casket at Love Field
Airport, still in the spatter of her pink suit
like the day we did paints in Mrs. Simon's class,
her stockings and her right glove caked
a darker shade.

Naming

In his garden, father packs the flower beds, protects
them from winter with burlap
and twine. He whistles and sings
"An English Country Garden"
and I follow along, reciting the lyrics –
Daffodils, heart's ease and flox
Meadowsweet and lady smocks
Gentian, lupine and tall hollihocks
Roses, foxgloves, snowdrops, blue forget-me-nots.

Then, he names the lilies
Lilium Auratum, Lilium Speciosum,
the Asiatic crossbreed Lilium Stargazer – and the roses –
Rosa Maiden's Blush,
Hybrid Tea, Hybrid Musk, plus
the pungent scented Buff Beauty and Penelope.

I like the nomenclature, a sub-rosa secret.
I lock the words away in my memory cabinet
with the study of reason and French verbs still conjugating.
I take them out when I need them –
words I'll whisper one day at his funeral –
when I need to be reminded
of father coming in from the garden, arms full
of clipped blooms which mother would place
in every room of the house.

Belle de Jour

Dancing after school at Carole Bryan's house,
high on milk cartons in our white go-go boots
with zips up the back, we are Sexy Sadies,
Solid Gold Dancers shaking and shimmying

in our fishnets and hot pants. At slumber parties
in our baby doll nighties, nursing bottles of coke,
we watch the *Ed Sullivan Show* –
the Beatles singing *She loves you, yeah, yeah, yeah*

and I wanna hold your hand
and Mick doing his bump and grind
in Ed's censored version
of "Let's Spend the Night Together."

We strut through the house, Motown divas
vamping to "Stop in the Name of Love" –
we perfect the gestures, hands cupping our hair,
up to our elbows in white evening gloves.

Late at night, we watch old movies
in which Deneuve, as Séverine,

bats false eyelashes above a white
push-up bra, and Eva Marie Saint, as Edie,

drops her small white dress glove
which Marlon Brando, as Terry,
picks up and pulls onto
his brute boxer's paw.

Leap, 2007

White Nightshirt, 2008

Wild Thing

Giant daisies grow along the walls of my room
as I listen to Dylan's "All Along the Watchtower,"
Outside in the distance a wildcat did growl,
Two riders were approaching and the wind began to howl.

Morrison sings "Light my Fire,"
then Hendrix in a purple haze, butanes
the varnish from his electric guitar, crackling
"Wild Thing" from the cream leather casing
of my Grundig radio.

In my room, the white sleeve of The Beatles.
George's guitar gently weeping.
Gracie's Alice and the White Rabbit.
Nights in white satin.
A whiter shade of pale.

(Everything feels rare as ivory.)

Cherries in the Snow

When my parents go out,
I reach into mother's
bureau drawer,
the top one

as tall as me
and wind myself in the white
silk scarf father bought her in Paris,
and roll on her Revlon Cherries

in the Snow lipstick.
Then, I dab perfume on strap lines
that cut across my brown skin

like trails of fighters
curving away from the cauterized part

of Viet Nam
they just firebombed

on the news

in the family room.

Silk Slip, 2008

25

White Gloves, 2008

Mission Apollo

At neighbourhood cocktail parties,
women in hostess caftans
serve pigs-in-blankets and highballs,
while we spin our vinyl
and make out
on perfumed coat piles in master bedrooms.

On TV, Technicolor men tout
stars in convertibles –
astronauts and their white-gloved wives waving,
McNamara's voice babbling,
the naked napalmed girl running
down the highway, skin in ribbons.

Choreography

In the library, among the stacks and card catalogues
with tiny wooden drawers of secret worlds,
I'm in love with transport, the gilt pages
of runaway children, women in heavy silks.

At home in my room, the stacks of overdue books
beside my bed harden into steppes.
My eyes cross them like locomotives carrying
Lara and Yuri through the Urals of *Dr. Zhivago*,
ice crystals on windows. Nabokov's blue butterflies
flit across the room as I read Montaigne,
the poems of Verlaine, mother's *Chatelaine*.

Outside, the sounds of traffic flow
into the night and in my mind
the rivers of the St. Lawrence, and the Volga
intermingle their waters. I waltz
the waltz from *War and Peace* amidst the clang
of closed lockers in the hallways of Beaconsfield High.

In the kitchen, mother hums through a clatter of dishes
and reports of massacres in Cambodia.
In the sharp smell of Chekhov's cherry orchards I turn
the pages, volume by volume, to stay my departure.

Blue Butterflies, 2007

29

Black and White, 2008

Soundtracks

Summers I lifeguard at the pool,
blue as a canvas by Hockney.
Weekends I iron my hair
like Ali McGraw in *Love Story*,
dab Eau de Love or Love's Baby Soft
on my temples, between my breasts.
My California boy and I
in his father's Buick.
Above his heart, a scar I bless
with my mouth, my hands,
as hands reach through the radio
strumming us to
"Sunshine of My Love" and
"Don't You Want Somebody to Love,"
hands in long white gloves,
divas singing *baby love oh baby love.*

I learn more
as I lie with my first love
in our first room,
his other scars,
his knees and palms,

while Clapton sings
in a white room with black curtains
where shadows run from themselves.
I like to imagine it was like this
for mother and father –
making me in a cool room,
in a bed of heat.

Pilgrimage

Mouth studded with pins,
mother sews my prom dress
the print peeled from
one of her cotton saris.

A pattern of roses
parts at the neck
exposing my skin
to the devotions
of boys bearing corsages.

On prom night
we drink tequila sunrises
and pink ladies, in our mothers'
borrowed pearls.
We climb the trail
to Mount Royal.
Above us, in Saint Joseph's Oratory,
a priest once offered me
the body of Christ
and the basilica rang
with organs.

The Votive Chapel,
ablaze with white candles,
was full of crutches, canes, and braces
left by the healed.

But now we dance
to Zeppelin's "Stairway to Heaven"
and morning birdsong
as the sun rises
scarlet over Montréal.

Libretto

They are shooting
Kennedy and King and Bobby.

Others are shooting
up, the boys on leave.
They're leaving
dogtags in the bars of Saigon
and the whore-houses of Hanoi –
their hob-nail boots with the National Trust.

The National Guard are shooting
their own. Four dead in Ohio.

The KKK in their white robes
and masks are blowing
up four young girls
during Sunday service
at the Birmingham Sixteenth Street Baptist.

Motor City is burning
and Newark too exploding
under acetylene skies.

And the lynched are singing

And Beatles are singing
over the sitar.

And Simon and Garfunkel are singing
sounds of silence.

And soldiers in Nam are watching
water hyacinth
float along the Mekong after the rains.
They are humming
in jungle woods
an anthem by The Youngbloods
Darkness, darkness be my pillow
Take my head and let me sleep
In the coolness of your shadow
In the silence of your deep

We won't get fooled again.

Ashes of Roses, 2002

2

Take this waltz, take this waltz,
Take its broken waist in your hands.

—Leonard Cohen, "Take This Waltz (After Lorca)"

Glory Days

These things must still be there —

our first rented apartment,
the old walk-up on an elm-lined street,
the landlord's naugahyde couch,
the clawfoot tub and the cat,
our imprints on the old iron bed
with the busted springs,

the farmer's market and the pub,
the Old Chestnut Inn, where they serve
apple pie with rum and cheddar,
where Stan Rogers' maritime ballads
mellow the oak walls,

beer at the Riverside Arms,
tea in Penny's kitchen,
midnight feasts of Chinese food and
club sandwiches at The Diplomat,

your baby blue Volkswagon van,

windows flowered with your mother's curtains,
the rough tympani
of the cancered-out muffler,

the boys smoking dope, doing hot knives,
listening to Jackson Browne and J. J. Cale,
the girls strutting to "Staying Alive," dancing to Donna
Summer, discoing to "Saturday Night Fever,"

the stoned haze of sweet crazed hours,
our imagined plan for the heist of the Dali
at the Lord Beaverbrook Gallery.

August Wedding: Anand Karaj

Nothing is really lost. Take this white wedding
in the steepled church. After vows, stretch limos
slide down Saturday streets with cargoes of chiffoned
bridesmaids. At the reception, the bride and groom pray
for rosary miracles, drink the marriage wine,
release doves into the sky – covenants against broken hallelujahs.

Or take Veronese's "Wedding at Cana," the huge
canvas we saw in Paris – carnival courtyard
with its Doric and Corinthian columns,
musicians playing lutes and viola da gamba,
the dwarf holding a parrot –
Jesus and his mother haloed
under the butchered lamb,
guests with their goblets of wine and when
the wine runs out, Jesus turning the water into wine.

Years ago, restless before another wedding.
Our jeans slipped off,
sari slung across your suited sleeve,

we enter my childhood home.
No bridal white or Indian red for me –
but a pale pink in between.
My aunties dress me, pleat lengths
of silk into my petticoat. I never learned
the art of the sari
and the heavy gold of Indian brides
weighs too much for me.
Just the single bracelet custom-made
for my small wrist
by distant hands in Delhi.

Among women in saris, turbaned sirdars,
Liberals, immigrants, and those
who will vote for Trudeau's white papers,
we marry.
For mother and father and relatives in India
father places the end of your *pulla* in my hand –
garments joined, you lead me, guided by father,
uncles, cousin, as if I might not find my way.
I am led by men in rings
around the book of scriptures,
the *Guru Granth Sahib*. Four times
around in the *Char Lavan*, ragas
sung with tabla and harmonium,

hymns and prayers in a mother tongue
foreign to me.

The relief on your Scottish
mother's face at the second ceremony
when we are double-ringed in English.
The minister's voice *let us pray* in witness
and blessing and Holy Kiss and Amen –
I take you we recite, standing in awe,
not in belief of witness or covenant
but in ceremony – our bodies wed already,
vows whispered stronger than prayers
memorized and chanted.

Outside the church,
we are garlanded with flowers,
showered with petals.
At the reception,
I toss my clutch of orchids and roses
ribbons streaming into my sister's
outstretched hands.

Years later, we're in the album –
I thought it was lost –
but there we are under vellum.

I dance with father to "All You Need is Love."
On the next page, I've spun away
and across the floor to
the hook of your arm.

Nothing is really lost.
We pass the steepled church each day,
each of us separate, in and out of love
with the music of that long ago hour
when there is always a wedding, our own vows
sparking fire when the wine is drained from the cup.

Hush

All winter in stucco on 65th I learned to love
what couldn't speak: what began in milk and

blood. Baby, cat, the man who worked long weeks
away from home. Forty below. My breath before me,

snow stiff trees burlapped against processions of
storms. I shoveled walks, plugged the car into a

block heater. Nursed the baby, fed the cat. Waited
for the man I was slow to love. Sometimes I'd ride the

bus to the bistro, only place in town that served espresso –
let it flow bitter down my throat – the bistro where Czech

brothers in white shirts and black trousers knew all about the
baby, the cat, the man I was slow to love.

At home, in quiet, I folded laundry, changed the baby's
diapers, fed the cat, watched backyards fill with snow.

In spring, green pushing through sidewalk cracks,

I woke, pressed my mouth to your back —

you — whom I was slow to love. And bed and house
smelled forever of me falling suddenly into love, rappelling

the past in a blaze through decades of renovations, creak
of floorboards, families coming and going, ledgers of forgotten

bills, tables laid for supper, someone waving on a front porch,
new brides, the washing of the dead, all the stories

I never wrote about us, your arms around the baby,
around me, sealed into cracked plaster with a kiss.

Dream of Billie

In a bar hung with smoke, she smooths her
white satin dress over her hips, pulls
her evening gloves over
the curves of her elbows.
She runs her tongue along the bars
of "Strange Fruit."
Then she turns to me and says:
you can be in white satin, with gardenias
in your hair and no sugar cane for miles,
but you can still be working on a plantation.

High fever for days
the dream keeps me company.
Between worlds, I am plural –
I still hear Billie, her ravaged gravel
dream a little dream of me
over the steel of a streetcar
rattling my window.
In the milk light of morning,
my eyes focus and notice
the fine hairs on your arms,
the whites of your eyes
I realize you've held me
for hours, jazz cooling
the viral nights.

Lucy, 2008

49

Prayer, 1999

Campo Santo

You have spent all your blue in these streets of metaphor—
Desire, Piety, Pleasure.

You have used up the memory of
lumps of canebreak along the four
laner from Mobile to Mississippi
miles of lowland and bayou
where hustlers and leather boys gather,
all the way to tracks, the Mississippi River
and remnants of slate roofs slumping to powder.
Headsuckers, rosary prayers,
maskers – three hundred years
of disease and high waters.

Drink your chicory in white cups
in the rancid rot and fetid filigree.
Remember the days
of Congo Square
when slaves were allowed
to gather Sundays
to cut the bodies
loose.

(In the hollow neighborhoods
little girls chant
Fix the levee,
Fix the levee.)

You have found Christ
everywhere – bronzed beside piles
of toys
and dogs rooting through piles
of garbage
in gutted houses.

You have found some things
keep – herons returning
to Audubon Park,
dogs' barks,
the Creole wail of zydeco streets –
accordions and frottoirs –
the stubborn magnolias and roses.

What Begins Bitterly

Small talk in coffee shops.
An hour or a century clip-clops
by, fragile after argument.

Rain over the Hudson, your hair beaded with drops.
How the river accepts everything – bears away flyers
like flung bouquets. Along the walkway, joggers and dogs,
circus tent where trapeze artists fly and pitch
lessons to those who always wanted to fly.

Crepuscule sky bleeds orange, gilding the already
orange taxis gaudy. On an uptown streetcorner,
a woman wears small bones around her neck,
chatters to red-tailed hawks circling, lending
the skyscrapers living gargoyles or spreading wings
over the Park where we traversed February ice
at the pace of monks, small talk flagging
by the Gates of Christo and Jean Claude –
prayer flags the color of Buddhist robes.

We were here once, years ago.
On the windshield, rain spitting.

On the radio, Marianne Faithful spitting
"Broken English." Umbilical cord dragged across
burial grounds. Sheets of sex and cigarettes.
I, too, would dress in satin for absolution.
Midnight at the Chelsea Hotel.
We came for beauty,
tongues pierced with hallelujah.

Courtyard drift of jazz. In the music playing,
every place we've been –
every June too. Every moment you
were, to me, that one thing
shining. In the music playing,
our living and our dying.
In this crowded room,
without moving a hand,
I touch you.

Black Shoes, 2008

Evening Fields VII, 2002

Augustine Said

We talk about art.
How this or that
              painting or poem or sonata could still move
                        you.

How year after year that
              still-life or symphony or sonnet still makes
                     you
ache to touch it.

———

We talk about art
into the night.
Above the houses
the moon, halfway through its phases, paints
                     the porch silver.
In the flesh of my hand – your hand, your all
                  I need
                  and know.

If art is private religion, so too love. We take it all
                  to heart as if,

Augustine said,
our existence depends
upon the pumping of it.

———

We talk about art
as the long slow walk leads us back along streets
                              to each other.
We don't notice snow falling on snow. Our arms are full of each other's
                              ache of spirit for the other's
                              matter.
Without art, the world snaps shut, clams
up. We need clay, chords. Cellos can't bow
                              of their own accord.

Adagio

When father dies,
mother packs up the moon and stars.
She commits to the task of grief,
paces the half-dreamt rooms,
continues to punch the clock at the public library –
lost in books and sounds
of silence.

Outside in the garden of flowers
father named, spring's plaque of blooms,
maimed birches.
I clip rain battered stalks
of white lilacs and iris.
I climb a tree like I did as a girl.
Perched in the weeping willow,

I dream of waking
in the wood of true stories.

Meanwhile, in the rubble
of the burned library in Sarajevo,
the cellist plays Albinoni's "Adagio in G Minor"
for twenty two days, for twenty two
killed waiting in a breadline.

The scroll of his cello
is a fist shaken in the face
of death.

Evening Fields II, 2002

Daughters, 2008

Elegy

Now in our daughters' empty rooms,
the neural storms of their mother.
Our girls lie down with lovers,
each girl's face
my own.
I hear a trace
of their grandfather's lullabies
Soja, Raj Kumari, soja –
Sleep, Princess, sleep.

On the stereo the Stones' "Paint it Black,"
U2's *Rattle and Hum,*
The Band's last waltz, "Helpless Helpless."

But I listen for strains
of father singing
along to Punjabi and Hindi ghazals

or Roger Whittaker –
moi j'ai quitter mon pays bleu –
as he slices oranges for me in morning
as I fold the starched turban
he wears for work in laboratories.

And I see him walking away
down the front lawn's
path like a part
in hair,
humming
with Harry Belafonte:

I'm sad to say, I'm on my way
Won't be back for many a day
My heart is down, my head is turning around
I had to leave a little girl in Kingston town.

Nightline

Friday April 30, 2004

Tonight Koppel reads
not the news copy
but name after name
of the Americans killed
in Iraq since March 19, 2003 –
military branch, rank, age
displayed on the screen,
names recited without music,
and I think of Cronkite reading
the names of the dead years ago,
filling our family room with names,
and I think of that time
in front of the Vietnam Memorial,
that silent slab of black stone,
how I swore I would not,
but wept anyway
at the engraved way
the names begged
to be traced
by fingers
as if the minds
of 58,022 dead
were ambered there.

Give us this day

our daily bread, we recited in unison, asking forgiveness
for our trespasses without knowing the meaning of trespass.
And lead us not into temptation, we chanted. *But deliver us from evil.*
For thine is the kingdom, and the power, and the glory,
for ever and ever. Over and over, led by teacher, our repetitions scoured
prayers into the earth's surface like wind, rain, thunder.
Day after day, yellow buses carried their charges
back to waiting mothers. Night after night, lovers kneeled
to each other as to no other. But now after
decades, a headline of Amish schoolgirls line up against a chalkboard
for execution by bullet. We steady ourselves bone
by bone, stand vigil for the ruined schoolyards.
And I start each day, kneeling to you as to no other. I lead
my classroom, wash the black slate clean while they read.

New Year's Eve

A band plays the blues. A small girl boogies
with her mother, party dress a crinoline twirl, boots
and tights humming, tiara halo shining over her grin.
And we dance – you hold me against your body
in the aftermath of savagery, massacres, disasters.
Scorched schoolyards, torture, butchery.
The world splits over and over.
Outside the windows, snow insists. Drifts.
The singer with the low whiskey voice slow dances
us into the new century. Torch-songed.

Dream of a Little Breakfast

In my dream my father brings me tea on a tray,
chota hazari in the early hours of morning,
like the servant in his boyhood –
tea poured in white china cups
boiled milk under wrinkled skin.

I ask him to stay. I want to hear his voice.
Some canticle or ghazal or lullaby
or even "White Christmas."
But I know this is not a hill station.
This is not his beloved Simla.
It is winter in Ontario, the only sound

a footfall crunch across frosted fields.

Evening Fields V, 2002

Embrace, 2008

Ain't No Cure

I slice oranges in the kitchen.
The countertop worn, notched
with the story of the knife.

I've been reading Ovid's *Cure for Love.*
You circle my waist with your arms –
kiss the back of my neck.
I remember who we were –
the taste of us sweet and dangerous
the girl and boy on the front porch
cooling our heels on our way
to the grave.

We believed we could make something
in the dark.

Stop-time

At times I've travelled far from you –
brought to my knees by want
in white rooms in distant cities
and always, music phantoms me –
fevered, carnal –
the rock and roll of my youth,
the blues of Clapton and B. B. King,
the jazz dark and peeling,
Miles and Monk and Billie,
the straight statements of gospel,
Mahaliah Jackson's every note a prayer
that reaches me for brief instants,
after dinner at Frederick's and Robert's
where gulls were circling,
seven settings of the sun sliding into English Bay.
I stood under the catalpa tree that sang white blossoms onto my hair
and through my fingers and I was home.
Blackbirds in the milk-blue light before dawn
scoring the silence.
Stop-time on the wet embouchure of a trumpet.
Music waiting in a white room,
white on white playing on
in the rabid world, and I your winter queen, your one and only.

Evening Fields VI, 2002

Notes and Discography

Epigraph to 1. Lyrics from "All Along the Watchtower," Bob Dylan, on the album *John Wesley Harding*, Columbia Records, 1967.

"Journey." India gained independence from the British Empire in 1947. The subsequent Partition, which created the two independent states of India and Pakistan, was followed by one of the most violent and bloody migrations and ethnic cleansings in history. The religious fury unleashed caused the deaths of some two million Hindus, Muslims, and Sikhs. An estimated 12 to 15 million people were forcibly transferred between the two countries.

"Naming." Lyrics from "An English Country Garden," Jimmie Rodgers. Performed on the album of the same title, Columbia Records, 1961.

"Belle de Jour." The Rolling Stones, in their appearance on the *Ed Sullivan Show* in 1967, performed a censored version of "Let's Spend the Night Together." The conditions of their appearance were that they were not to sing the title or repeat it during their performance. The lyrics were changed to: "Let's Spend Some Time Together." The poem also refers to the films *Belle de Jour*, 1967, directed by Luis Bunuel and *On the Waterfront*, 1954, directed by Elia Kazan.

"Wild Thing." Lyrics from "All Along the Watchtower," by Bob Dylan on the album *John Wesley Harding*, Columbia Records, 1967.

"Soundtracks." Lyrics to "Baby Love," by Brian Holland, Lamont

Dozier, and Edward Holland, Jr. performed by The Supremes on the album *Where Did Our Love Go?* Motown Records, 1964. This poem also makes reference to Eric Clapton and the song "White Room," by Pete Brown Jack Bruce, recorded by Cream on Disc One of the double album *Wheels of Fire*, Atlantic Studios, 1968.

"Libretto." The poem refers to the Klu Klux Klan bombing of the 16th Street Baptist Church in Birmingham, Alabama, Sept. 15, 1963. Four young girls were killed: Denise McNair, age 11; Cynthia Wesley, age 14; Carole Robertson, age 14, and Addie Mae Collins, age 14. Lyrics from "Darkness, Darkness." Jesse Colin Young and the Youngbloods. *Elephant Mountain*, RCA Records, 1969. During the Vietnam War the song was considered an "anthem" by American soldiers for it described what they felt during combat in the jungles. Lyrics to "Won't Get Fooled Again," by Pete Townshend. Performed by The Who on the album *Who's Next*, Polydor Records(UK) MCA Records (USA). First released as a single, 7" 45rpm format, 1971.

Epigraph to Section 2. Lyrics from "Take This Waltz (After Lorca)," by Leonard Cohen on the album *I'm Your Man*, Sony/ATV Music,1988. Published in *Stranger Music: Selected Poems and Songs*. Toronto: McClelland and Stewart, 1993.

"August Wedding: Anand Karaj." *Anand Karaj* is the Sikh wedding ceremony, meaning Blissful Ceremony or Occasion. The *Char Lavaan*, are four ragas or stanzas, called *Shabads*, which are read and then sung during the ceremony. *Pulla* is the scarf worn by the bridegroom. The ceremony is held in the presence of the *Guru Granth Sahib*, the Sikh holy scripture, written in *Gurmukhi* script. The poem also refers to Italian painter Paolo Veronese's "The Wedding at Cana," oil on canvas, 1563, at the Musée du Louvre, Paris.

"Dream of Billie." Italicized quote is commonly attributed to Billie Holiday.

"Adagio." The cellist in the poem is based on the story of Vedran Smailović, known as the "Cellist of Sarajevo," a former Principal Cellist of the Sarajevo Opera. In Sarajevo, in 1992, 22 people were killed when mortar fire exploded in the marketplace while they queued for bread. In response to the massacre, amidst the mortar fire and sniper's bullets, Smailović played Albinoni's "Adagio in G Minor" on his cello for 22 days to honour the dead. Albinoni's Adagio, arranged by Remo Giazotto, was first published in 1958. Jim Morrisson and The Doors recorded the Adagio on their studio album, *An American Prayer*, in 1978, Elektra records.

"Elegy." Lyrics from "Mon Pays Bleu," Roger Whittaker (French version of Durham Town), EMI Records, 1969. Lyrics from "Jamaica Farewell," Harry Belafonte, *Calypso*, RCA Records, original release 1955.

"*Give us this day*" refers to the shootings of Amish schoolgirls at West Nickel Mines School, Lancaster County, Pennsylvania, October 2, 2006.

This poem is for the girls who were murdered: Naomi Rose Ebersol, age 7 years; Marian Stoltzfus Fisher, age 13 years; Lena Zook Miller, age 7 years; Mary Liz Miller, age 8 years, and Anna Mae Stoltzfus, age 12 years.

Notes on the Art

Pg. 5 – *Prayer*, acrylic on panel, 36" x 36", 2002

Pg. 11 – *Molting Rose*, acrylic and phototransfer on canvas, 16" x 16", 2007

Pg. 12 – *Molting Petals*, acrylic and phototransfer on canvas, 16" x 16", 2007

Pg. 21 – *Leap*, mixed media on wood panel, 36" x 24", 2007

Pg. 22 – *White Nightshirt*, acrylic and graphite on wood panel, 48" x 36", 2008

Pg. 25 – *Silk Slip*, acrylic and graphite on canvas, 48" x 72", 2008

Pg. 26 – *White Gloves*, acrylic and graphite on wood panel, 36” x 48”, 2008

Pg. 29 – *Blue Butterflies*, mixed media on canvas, 12" x 12", 2007

Pg. 30 – *Black and White*, acrylic and charcoal on canvas, 48" x 60", 2008

Pg. 37 – *Ashes of Roses*, acrylic and charcoal on canvas, 36" x 36", 2002

Pg. 49 – *Lucy*, mixed media on wood panel, 48" x 36", 2008

Pg. 50 – *Prayer*, acrylic and graphite on canvas, 36" x 36", 1999

Pg. 55 – *Black Shoes,* acrylic and charcoal on canvas, 48" x 72", 2008

Acknowledgements

My thanks to poets Paul Muldoon, Mark Doty, Glyn Maxwell, and Kathleen Graber, for their readings and responses to some of these poems. Sincere thanks to Jason Guriel, for his fine editing skills, thoughtful critiques, and conversations about this manuscript. Thanks also to Priscila Uppal and Russell Thornton for editorial and creative support. A special note of thanks to Jamie Ross and Joe Paczuski for caring sustenance through the writing and for generous readings and insightful suggestions.

Thanks to the editors of publications in which some of these poems appeared. "Hush" was first published in *Blackbird*. "Augustine Said" was published in *In Praise of Poeisis: The Arts and Human Existence*, edited by Ellen Levine and Paul Antze.

I am grateful to The University of British Columbia, Centre for Cross-Faculty Inquiry, for the opportunity to pursue my work on this manuscript as Poet in Residence in 2006-2007. Thanks to Rob Tierney, Graeme Sullivan, and Lynn Fels.

I would also like to express my immense gratitude to Linda Lando, owner of LindaLando Fine Art, Vancouver, BC, for her support of this publication and for my artistic collaborations with Suzanne Northcott over the years. *White Album* was launched in 2008 as part of Suzanne Northcott's exhibition Lucid Ground, at LindaLando Fine Art. Thanks also to Liane Davison, curator of the Surrey Public Art Gallery, for her ongoing support of our collaborations.

Excerpts from this manuscript were included in an invited keynote lecture titled "Tender Music: Narrative, Cadence, and the Force of Events," at the Narrative Soundings Conference on Narrative Inquiry in Music Education at Herberger College of Fine Arts, School of Music, Arizona State University, February 8, 2008. Thanks to Sandy Stauffer and Margaret Barrett for their gracious invitation.

—*Rishma Dunlop*

I would like to express my thanks for the extraordinary community of artists surrounding me. They joyfully offered themselves as models for some of the works in this collection, took the photos for my self portrait work and supported me in endless ways. At the risk of missing as many as I mention, thanks to Janice Robertson, Judy Nygren, Maya Grillo York Masser, Linda Siemens, Billie-jo Thomson, Kaaiser Sethna, Cara Dunlop, Rachel Dunlop, Robert Genn, and Reinier DeSmit. My deep thanks, too, to my dear friend and art dealer Linda Lando for years of encouragement and support.

—*Suzanne Northcott*

Rishma Dunlop and Suzanne Northcott.
Photo: Joe Paczuski

Rishma Dunlop is a Canadian poet, playwright, essayist, and fiction writer. She is the author of three previous books of poetry: *Metropolis, Reading Like a Girl,* and *The Body of My Garden.* Books as editor include: *White Ink: Poems on Mothers and Motherhood* and *Red Silk: An Anthology of South Asian Canadian Women Poets.* She is the recipient of numerous awards and grants, including the Emily Dickinson Prize for Poetry, and she has been a finalist for the CBC Literary Prize in Poetry. Born in India, Dunlop was raised in Beaconsfield, Quebec. She is a professor at York University, Toronto, where she is Coordinator of the Creative Writing Program in English.

Suzanne Northcott is an interdisciplinary artist working with installation, video, painting and drawing. Themes of isolation and connection are woven through her history of collaborative work with poets, scientists and artists in other genres. Northcott's art is widely exhibited and found in private, corporate and public gallery collections, including The Surrey Art Gallery permanent collection. Awards include the McIvor Bentall award and the Spillsbury Bronze medal. Northcott has lived in historic Fort Langley, BC, since 1996.

Marquis Book Printing Inc.

Québec, Canada

2008